When the Dream Changes

Loving Through Disappointment

A Three-Part Journey Through Love, Clarity, and Peace

FATIMA ANNE

Dedication

For the woman who stayed and found herself anyway.
And for the ones watching her become.

—Fatima Anne

Acknowledgment

To my family,

Thank you for being part of a journey that shaped me, challenged me, and ultimately brought me back to myself.

Everything I've built, I carry with you in mind.

Author's Note

There comes a point in every woman's life when the noise gets too loud and even your own reflection starts to sound like someone else.

I wrote this piece for that moment, the one where peace stops being a quote on the internet and starts calling your name for real.

The Peace Practice was born out of my own quiet unraveling. The kind that doesn't announce itself, it just shows up in the mornings, and you can't find your energy. The conversations that leave you empty. The mirror that looks familiar but feels foreign. I didn't need another "self-help" book. I needed a soft homecoming.

So I built one, page by page.

Disappointment taught me honesty. Clarity taught me boundaries. Peace taught me how to breathe again.

This isn't something you rush through; it's something you grow through. You might read it daily, or only when the silence gets too heavy. You might cry on a few pages, or laugh at how far you've come. Either way, I want you to know: you don't need to be "fixed." You're just returning. Return to your softness. Return to your rhythm. Return to your peace, the one that was always yours.

When the dream changes, let it. When the silence feels like loss, sit with it. And when you finally start to hear yourself again, answer.

Welcome home.

— Fatima Anne

When the Dream Changes

Loving Through Disappointment

PART ONE

Grief. Disappointment. Emotonal Truth

"When the dream changes, let it.
What's meant to stay will find peace here."

The Blueprint

"We built the dream together until one of us stopped believing."

The living room table was always your boardroom.

Scraps of paper, dreams half-drawn in pen, the smell of ambition thick in the air. You were both younger and hungrier. Him sketching menus for the catering company, you mapping out how the brand would grow, how the boys would one day inherit something with their names on it. You called it legacy work. He called it something he was good at.

The nights stretched long and easy back then. You'd talk about dreams and how big they could be. You'd argue over fonts and colors for the logo, then collapse into laughter, your fingers stained with ink and purpose. Back then, you believed in the "we" more than the "me." You didn't know how heavy that would become.

The Shift Begins

Years later, that same table is quieter. There are bills where the dreams used to sit. He still loves you, you can feel it, but it's like the love has grown stale, old, stiff in its knees, uninterested in dancing anymore. He says he's tired. You're tired too, but yours is the kind that burns. You're still building, still fighting, still believing that maybe if you just tweak the plan again, you can revive the blueprint.

But the truth hits slowly: You can't revive what someone stopped believing in.

The Anatomy of a Shared Dream

Dreams built in partnership have two fragile parts, vision and agreement. When one fades, the other starts to crumble. The blueprint was never just about the business or the house. It was about belonging. About feeling like you were walking toward the same horizon. Now you're standing at that same horizon, wondering why it feels so lonely.

Soul Note

Maybe the hardest part of disappointment isn't when love dies, maybe it's when you realize it's just not working the same way. You're both still breathing, but the dream isn't. And no matter how strong you are, there's mourning in that.

REFLECTION PROMPTS FOR THE READER:

What dream did you build together that no longer feels mutual?

____

____

____

How did you first start noticing the shift?

____

____

____

Which parts of the dream still belong to you, even if they no longer belong to us?

____

____

____

Affirmation

"I can honor what we built without clinging to what's no longer growing."

The Shift You Didn't See Coming

"It didn't break in one night. It bent until I couldn't tell where the dream ended and the denial began."

It started so small you didn't even name it. Long hours at someone else's establishment. Him working late, then too tired to talk when he got home. And when he did talk he gave even shorter answers.

At first, you told yourself it was stress and the growing pains of life. You'd pour a drink, scroll through old photos, and whisper, "We've been through worse." But worse wasn't what this was. This was indifference disguised as peace.

He wasn't cruel, just... gone in spirit. Still there physically, still providing, still smiling for the family photos, but the energy between you two, that thick, sacred thread that used to hum with connection, was slowly unraveling, day by day.

You noticed it in the way he'd kiss your cheek instead of your lips. In the way you started turning on your side before he did. In how "I love you" became background noise, not music. The dream was shifting, and it felt like you were the only one trying to hold it still.

The Slow Fade

There's a special kind of loneliness that comes from being partnered but unseen. You start to miss the "us", while the "you" starts fading too.

You try to talk about it, softly at first. "Do you think we're okay?" He says, "yes." without looking up. And in that moment, you realize he thinks this version is fine.

You stop asking. You start over-functioning instead, overcooking, over-earning, over-loving, over-explaining. Trying to prove to the universe that you can carry both your dream and his disinterest on your own shoulders. But love isn't proof. And you can't build a legacy on silence.

How Distance Grows

Distance rarely happens from one big betrayal. It happens from a thousand small moments where two people stop reaching at the same time. He stopped reaching because he thought you'd never stop. You stopped reaching because you got tired of holding out empty hands.

Soul Note

Sometimes the shift isn't about who changed first, it's about who noticed it and who pretended not to. That noticing hurts like heartbreak, because it's the first time you see the love, without the illusion. But noticing is also the beginning of power.

REFLECTION PROMPTS FOR THE READER:

What small moments made you realize something had shifted?

____

____

____

How have you been over-functioning to fill emotional gaps?

____

____

____

When was the last time your partner reached for you, not just routine?

____

____

____

Affirmations

"I honor what's shifting, even when it hurts. I no longer call confusion love."

The Rooms We Don't Talk In

"It's amazing how quiet love can be when no one's listening anymore."

You can feel it before you even notice it, the hush that sits heavy between you two. It's not the peaceful kind of silence, the one that happens when love is steady and secure. It's the kind that hums with absence.

You move through the house like it's a museum of your old joy, each room holding a memory that doesn't match the mood anymore. The living room where you once danced with the boys to old-school jams now feels too clean, too still. The bedroom that used to smell like shea butter and laughter now smells like sleep and routine. You walk around, turning off lights you didn't turn on, metaphors everywhere, and you can't escape them. He's there, but you miss him anyway.

The Unspoken Rules of the Quiet House

You start to develop a rhythm that protects the silence instead of breaking it. Mornings become transactional. "Good morning" is a courtesy, not a connection. Dinner becomes background noise to whatever's playing on the TV.

Even disagreements get quieter, not because there's peace, but because arguing feels pointless when you already know you'll be unheard. You realize the worst kind of distance isn't physical. It's emotional exile inside your own home.

Emotional Labor in the Shadows

Every household has invisible labor. Cooking, cleaning, planning, scheduling, that's the visible part. But the real exhaustion comes from the emotional labor:

- Remembering birthdays,
- Holding space for his stress,
- Protecting the kids from tension,
- Pretending you're okay.

You keep the family machine running while quietly unraveling. You know if you stop, everything will stop. So you keep moving, even when your soul begs for rest.

Soul Note

There's a special grief that comes from realizing that your silence has become survival. You stop asking to be heard because rejection is heavier than quiet. But here's the truth, silence might protect peace in the moment, but it poisons connection over time.

If you don't speak your truth, your body will. In headaches. In fatigue. In resentment. In weight you can't lose. Your heart starts to whisper, "I miss us." And the echo answers back, "So do I."

REFLECTION PROMPTS FOR THE READER:

Where in your life are you keeping silent to avoid discomfort?

____

____

____

What would happen if you spoke your truth gently but firmly?

____

____

____

What part of you goes quiet when you feel unheard?

____

____

____

Affirmation

"My silence is sacred when it protects my peace, not when it hides my pain."

Loving Someone Who Isn't Growing With You

"I kept waiting for him to catch up, not realizing I'd already walked too far."

Growth used to be your love language. You were both dreamers once, partners in progress, plotting the next move with late-night talks and shared ambition. But somewhere along the way, your growth started to look like pressure to him. Your excitement made him anxious. Your discipline made him defensive. Your drive reminded him of what he wasn't doing anymore.

And because you loved him, you dimmed yourself. You softened your tone, lowered your standards, shrank your joy, thinking maybe if you got smaller, the distance would shrink too.

But it didn't. It grew in silence. He started calling your evolution "extra." You started calling your pain "patience." And both of you got stuck in a cycle where love meant pretending that change wasn't necessary.

When Growth Becomes a Threat

You learned the hard way that some people don't leave; they just stop showing up at your level.

He's still there. He's still kind, funny at times, maybe even supportive in his on way. But he no longer builds with you, he just observes you. You're living side by side, but in different seasons. You're planting new seeds, he's still standing in last year's harvest. And it hurts because part of you wants to slow down, just so you can still walk beside him. But that's the trap: you can't grow and stay still at the same time.

The Fear of Outgrowing Love

Many of us are taught that "real love" means staying no matter what. But love isn't proof of loyalty, it's a living thing that needs oxygen, purpose, and movement. You're not leaving because you stopped loving him. You're grieving because you're starting to love yourself too.

Soul Note

You can't rescue someone from a comfort zone they've decorated to look like peace. And you can't keep shrinking to fit a space you were never meant to stay small in. The truth is, sometimes you're not asking for too much, you're just asking for it from the wrong version of them.

REFLECTION PROMPTS FOR THE READER:

In what ways have you dimmed your light to keep someone else comfortable?

____

____

____

What fears come up when you imagine growing beyond your partner?

____

____

____

How would your life look if you stopped apologizing for your evolution?

____

____

____

____

Affirmation

"My growth is not a threat, it's a blessing that reveals who's meant to rise with me."

The Grief of the Shared Dream

"We were supposed to build forever. No one warned me how quiet forever sounds when only one person's still working."

You don't notice when the dream dies. It doesn't slam the door or make an announcement. It just starts showing up less and less, until one day you wake up, and the dream you built together feels like a ghost living in your house.

You remember when everything was "one day." One day we'll own land. One day, Blu VI will have its own kitchen. One day we'll be free. But now "one day" has turned into "maybe," and "maybe" feels like "never."

He stopped talking about it. And at first, you took it personally. Then you took it as a challenge, doubling down on your hustle, pulling late nights, trying to keep the legacy alive by yourself. You wanted to prove that the dream could survive one person's exhaustion. But it couldn't. Dreams need two people believing, or they eventually suffocate under the weight of imbalance.

The Quiet Funeral

You've already had the funeral, you just didn't know it. It happened the night you looked at him while sitting on the couch and realized you were speaking two different languages.

He was talking about getting by. You were talking about building beyond. You didn't cry then. You just nodded and changed the subject because sometimes silence feels safer than explaining a dream to someone who no longer believes.

That night, you laid next to him, and the ache in your chest wasn't heartbreak; it was grief. Grief for the version of him who once dreamed in color with you. Grief for the version of you who believed that love alone could fund forever.

What Dying Dreams Teach Us

Grief doesn't always come from death, sometimes it comes from disconnection. And when you love deeply, you mourn quietly. You stop trying to make him dream. You stop trying to make him see. You start learning to build for yourself, and that, in its own way, is another kind of goodbye.

Soul Note

You are allowed to grieve the lifestyle, the plans, the promises. You are allowed to sit in that loss without guilt. Because what you're really mourning isn't failure, it's the version of life that once felt sacred and shared.

And here's the truth: The dream didn't die because you stopped believing. It died because you outgrew the version of yourself who needed someone else to believe it with you.

REFLECTION PROMPTS FOR THE READER:

What shared dream have you been keeping alive alone?

____

____

____

How have you tried to resurrect something that was never meant to survive?

____

____

____

Which parts of that dream can you reclaim and make your own?

____

____

____

____

Affirmation

"I can mourn what never became and still believe in what will."

Exercise: Releasing and Reclaiming

Column 1:

Dreams I'm Releasing (things that depended on "us").

Column 2:

Dreams I'm Reclaiming (things that belong to me now).

RELEASING	RECLAIMING
Building a business together	Expanding my own business my way
Buying a home as a couple	Creating a family home rooted in peace
Growing old in one story	Writing new chapters that still honor my legacy

RELEASING	RECLAIMING

The Decision to Stay

"I stayed, not because I was weak, but because I needed to understand what strength really looked like."

You could've left. God knows you've thought about it. There were nights when you sat in your car in the driveway, music low, eyes burning, just needing five minutes before walking into the house that doesn't feel like home anymore. But something deeper than fear or hope, something quieter held you still. It wasn't that you didn't know how to leave, it was that you weren't done building the foundation yet.

People love to romanticize leaving; the bags packed, the fresh start, and the freedom. But no one talks about the bravery of staying long enough to see the truth for what it really is. You decided to stay; not for him, not for comfort, but for clarity. Because you can't heal what you won't face.

The Difference Between Staying and Settling

There's a sacred difference between staying stuck and staying awake. One drains you. The other transforms you. You're staying with your eyes open now, tracking your patterns, watching his actions, studying your emotions like weather changes. You're no longer waiting for him to change. You're observing whether he wants to. You are your own witness now.

You pull out your notebook, not the one for business plans, but one for emotional inventory. You draw a line down the middle. One side says What's working. The other says What's not.

It's humbling how long the second list becomes. But instead of collapsing, you feel... awake because finally you're not running from the data of your own heart. You're collecting it. And that's where healing starts. This is your 90-Day Marriage Reset. It's not a punishment or a test, it's a mirror. A structured way to find truth in the mess.

Staying With Intention

Staying intentionally means:

- You're no longer begging.
- You're no longer pretending.
- You're no longer performing to avoid pain.

You're observing, and observation without expectation brings truth to the surface. You're learning whether this relationship can evolve with you or if it's simply the classroom for your next chapter.

Soul Note

You're not weak for staying. You're wise for knowing that clarity has its own timeline. You don't need to rush the revelation; you just need to stay long enough to know you won't repeat this version of love again. You can stay and still prepare. You can love and still let go. You can hope and still build an exit plan. Contradictions can coexist, that's what real womanhood looks like. Because two things can be true at once.

REFLECTION PROMPTS FOR THE READER:

Why am I staying; for fear, comfort, hope, or understanding?

____

____

____

What would I need to see to know this relationship can grow again?

____

____

____

What would I need to accept if it doesn't?

____

____

____

Affirmation

"I can stay without losing myself. I can wait without withering."

Exercise: The Clarity Chart

After completing it, readers note patterns; are they seeing effort, or excuses?

CATEGORY	WHAT'S WORKING	WHAT'S NOT
Communication	We talk daily, but not deeply	He avoids emotional topics
Partnership	We share bills	I do most of the parenting and planning
Intimacy	Occasional affection	Little emotional or physical closeness
Growth	I'm building new dreams	He's stuck in survival mode

CATEGORY	WHAT'S WORKING	WHAT'S NOT

Exercise: Mirror Check

Stand in front of a mirror; not for beauty, but for truth.

Say out loud:

- "This is what I've learned from loving him."
- "This is what I've learned about loving me."
- "This is what I refuse to repeat."

Write those sentences down. Read them every time you're tempted to doubt how far you've come.

____

____

____

____

____

____

____

____

____

____

____

The Mirror of Marriage

"He stopped being my mirror of love and became my mirror of truth."

It's late. The kids are asleep. The hum of the fridge fills the kitchen, that same kitchen that once held laughter, now holding tension you can't name. You catch a glimpse of yourself in the microwave door; tired eyes, robe half-tied, mind spinning with lists. And suddenly it hits you: this isn't just about him anymore.

It's about you. The you who stayed quiet to keep the peace. The you who watered a one-sided garden. The you who called patience, what it really was, fear. You realize this marriage hasn't just been showing you him. It's been reflecting you back to you.

The Mirror Doesn't Lie

Every relationship is a classroom, but marriage? Marriage is a house of mirrors. It shows you your best and your worst moments, your love and your limits.

He reflects your old wounds, the ones that crave validation. He mirrors your boundaries, the ones you bend too easily. He mirrors your growth, by showing you what happens when you stop pretending to be small. The mirror doesn't lie. It just waits for you to look long enough to tell the truth.

What the Mirror Shows

You start to see patterns and not to blame yourself, but to become free. You realize you've always been the fixer. The emotional translator. The peacemaker, even when you were breaking. And that role didn't start with him, it started way back. With the way you learned to love. With how you were taught to earn affection through effort. He's not the first reflection, he's just the clearest.

Soul Note

The mirror of marriage doesn't always show what's wrong with them. Sometimes it shows what's unfinished in you. And that's sacred work, not punishment, not karma, but a spiritual invitation to finally break your own cycle.

So now, when he dismisses your voice, you don't just see a careless partner; you see every time you silenced yourself to keep someone else comfortable. When he pulls away, you feel the echo of every time you over-gave just to be chosen. You're not reliving pain. You're revealing it, so you can finally release it.

REFLECTION PROMPTS FOR THE READER:

What patterns has your partner reflected back to you that you can now see clearly?

____

____

____

What old version of yourself do you keep becoming in this relationship?

____

____

____

What boundary, if honored, would change the way you show up in love?

____

____

____

Affirmation

"I can face what love reveals without losing who I am becoming."

The Self-Worth Reckoning

"When I stopped begging to be chosen, I remembered I already was."

You wake up one morning, and it's different. No dramatic argument. No sudden epiphany. Just quiet clarity. You look around the room; it's the same bed, the same man, the same routine, but the air feels lighter because you finally stopped waiting for validation to make you feel alive. You used to think his love was the prize. Now you see, it was supposed to be the partnership.

And the truth hits soft but deep: You forgot how powerful you were because you kept measuring your worth in his willingness.

The Moment of Reckoning

Self-worth doesn't return all at once; it arrives in whispers. It shows up the day you stop apologizing for your glow. The moment you realize you don't have to earn rest. The second you say no and don't explain why.

You start hearing your own voice again, the one that got buried under compromise and caretaking. She's been waiting, quietly rehearsing her comeback. This is her season

The Currency of Worth

When love becomes one-sided, it teaches you what you've been trading for peace: your time, your body, your joy, your ambition. But peace built on silence isn't peace, it's paralysis. Real worth says, "I can be soft without being small." It reminds you that your presence is a blessing, not a burden.

You start reclaiming your currency:

- Boundaries become your budget.
- Rest becomes your return.
- Joy becomes your profit.

Soul Note

He doesn't have to see your worth for it to multiply. You were divine before the disappointment. You were chosen before the chaos. You're not rebuilding, you're remembering. And when you finally remember who you are, you stop auditioning for the role of "enough."

REFLECTION PROMPTS FOR THE READER:

What have I been giving that was never mine to prove?

____

____

When did I start believing my value was negotiable?

____

____

____

What would my life look like if I treated myself like an investment?

____

____

____

Affirmation

"My worth isn't up for debate. I am the asset, the miracle, and the reward."

Exercise: The Worth Ledger

Write two lists:

Debits: places you've been emotionally or spiritually overdrawn.

Credits: actions, people, and habits that deposit energy back into you.

Then commit to balancing your emotional books.

Debits	Credits

Debits	Credits

The Soft Landing

"I stopped begging for safety and started building it."

There's a peace that comes when you stop waiting for someone to save you. One morning, you wake up and decide: I'm done living like I could lose everything at any moment. You open your notes app; not to vent, but to plan. You start listing the things that make you feel secure: a savings account, a calm space, a backup plan, a peace of mind. It's not a goodbye list. It's a "just in case I finally have to choose me" list. This is your Soft Landing. Not the fall. The flight.

What a Soft Landing Really Means

A Soft Landing is your quiet rebellion against dependency and fear. It's you whispering to your future, "Don't worry, I've got us." It's emotional and financial preparedness, not because you expect the worst, but because you deserve the best kind of peace: the kind that's non-negotiable.

You start creating soft spots for yourself everywhere:

- A friend you can stay with if you need space.

- A journal that holds your truth when you can't say it out loud.
- An emergency fund with your name on it.
- A daily affirmation that says, "I am my own safety net."

Love and Logistics

Love may be spiritual, but stability is strategic. And if you don't blend the two, you'll always feel powerless. A Soft Landing is how you honor both your heart and your head. It's how you protect your peace while still walking in faith and believing in your relationship. It's saying, "I don't know what will happen, but I refuse to be unprepared for my own freedom."

The Emotional Soft Landing

Start building emotional reserves the way you build savings:

- Rest without guilt.
- Reparent yourself when your inner child feels scared.
- Reach out when loneliness hits.
- Rehearse peace by creating daily moments of stillness that don't depend on anyone else's presence.

Emotional safety is the ground you land on when everything else shifts.

The Financial Soft Landing

Money doesn't solve heartbreak, but it softens the crash.
Build slowly, quietly, confidently.

GOAL	PLAN	TIMELINE
Create emergency fund	Save $25/week	6 months
Reduce Dependency	Open seperate account w/ auto deposit	Ongoing
Build confidence income	Freelance, uber, sell digitial product, etc.	Weekly Goal
Freedom fund	Label saving jar "Future ME" add excess	Now

GOAL	PLAN	TIMELINE

You don't have to leave to prepare. You just have to stop being afraid of what preparation means.

Soul Note

You can love him and still build a safety net. You can pray for change and still prepare for clarity. Faith without boundaries is just waiting, and you can't wait forever, at least you shouldn't.

A Soft Landing is how you make sure your love story, whatever direction it takes, still ends with you standing on your feet.

REFLECTION PROMPTS FOR THE READER:

What would a soft landing look like for me emotionally, financially, and spiritually?

____

____

____

What safety nets can I create that don't rely on my partner's participation?

____

____

____

What can I start doing this week that helps me sleep in peace, not fear?

____

____

____

____

Affirmation

"I don't have to fall apart to start over. My peace has a plan."

Exercise: The Soft Landing Plan

Break your life into these categories:

- Heart: Who helps me feel calm, safe, and grounded?
- Home: Where can I go if I need time or space?
- Money: What can I save, sell, or simplify to build security?
- Support: Who can I confide in without judgment?
- Soul: What routines or rituals bring me back to peace?

Fill in each category until your plan feels like a hug from your future self.

HEART				
HOME				
MONEY				
SUPPORT				
SOUL				

HEART				
HOME				
MONEY				
SUPPORT				
SOUL				

The Dream That's Still Yours

"I thought I lost everything when he stopped dreaming with me. But the truth is, the dream was waiting for me to remember it was mine all along."

You're driving alone one morning, no music, no destination, just silence and sky. The world feels still in that way it does after a storm, quiet but clean. You pull over for breakfast and catch your reflection in the window. For the first time in a long time, you like who you see. Not because everything's fixed, but because you're not pretending anymore. You survived the heartbreak of broken promises, the confusion of staying, the slow rebirth of remembering who you are. And somewhere along the way, you stopped needing him to catch the dream. You picked it up yourself.

Reclaiming the Vision

You start dreaming again, honestly. This time, the vision isn't tied to partnership; it's tied to purpose. The house, the business, the life you once built for "us", becomes the legacy you now build for you and everyone you love. You start expanding again. Not hustling from pain, but creating from peace. You stop performing survival and start practicing freedom.

What Remains After the Fire

After every loss, there's something left. It might not be what you expected, but it's pure, it's honest, it's you.

Here's what survived:

- Your ability to love deeply.
- Your faith, tested but intact.
- Your strength, finally untangled from struggle.
- Your clarity, the kind that doesn't flinch anymore.

You realize, the dream didn't die. It evolved. It shed the parts that required you to disappear. Now it's simpler, softer, smarter. Now it belongs fully to you; maybe it always did.

Soul Note

Peace doesn't come from perfect endings. It comes from aligned beginnings. You may never get the apology, the do-over, or the fairytale. But you got something way better, truth. And the truth, once accepted, will build you a new world.

This chapter isn't about what you lost. It's about the woman you became through loss. The dream still breathes through you is stronger, wiser, and finally free to grow without permission.

REFLECTION PROMPTS FOR THE READER:

What version of your dream do you want to rebuild for yourself?

____

____

____

What did this season teach you about what love should feel like?

____

____

____

How can you honor the past without living in it?

____

____

____

____

Affirmation

"The dream still belongs to me. And this time, I'm building it with peace as my partner."

Letters To The Dream

"Some things end so you can see what was always yours."

Maybe the dream didn't die, maybe it just evolved into something purer.

Something that doesn't need validation, or permission, or proof.

Maybe the dream was never "us."

Maybe the dream was me, finally remembering myself.

To the Life We Planned

"We were architects once. We drew forever with ink and good intentions."

Dear Dream,

We really tried, didn't we? We mapped out the house, the laughter, the legacy. We built on faith and adrenaline and the belief that love would always be enough to cover the cracks.

But somewhere along the way, the blueprint faded. The plans stayed taped to the wall, but the work stopped. And I kept building, hammer in hand, trying to keep the foundation from falling apart.

I forgive us both for not knowing how to grow the same way. You were still sacred, just not sustainable. Thank you for teaching me what a partnership can build. Thank you for showing me that I don't have to lose myself to hold love. You were the chapter that taught me how to dream with open eyes.

Goodbye, not with bitterness, but with gratitude.

Love,

Fatima Anne

To the Woman I Was

"You gave everything, and I mean everything, even the parts
you were supposed to keep."

Dear Me,

You did your best. Even when it wasn't enough for both of
you, it was still extraordinary.

You carried the house, the heart, the hope, and still
managed to show up smiling. I know you stayed longer than
you should've, not because you were weak, but because you
believed in healing more than you believed in endings. That
was love.

But now it's time for something new: peace without
performance.

You don't owe anyone smaller versions of yourself. You
don't need permission to start again. You are not the broken
woman in the story; you are the author who kept writing
even when it got dark.

Love,

Fatima Anne

To the Love That Taught Me Everything

"You were my favorite lesson and my hardest goodbye."

Dear Love,

You changed shape on me. You used to feel like a sunrise, now you feel like weather; unpredictable but familiar. I used to pray for you to come back the way you were. Now I just pray we both find peace where we are.

You taught me that real love doesn't always look like forever... sometimes it looks like release.

Thank you for the laughter.

Thank you for the mirror.

Thank you for the version of myself I met because of you.

We will always share a timeline, but maybe not a trajectory.

And that's okay.

Love,
Fatima Anne

To the Peace That Found Me Anyway

"You came quietly. Not as a person, but as a presence."

Dear Peace,

You didn't arrive with fireworks. You showed up in small ways...

... in mornings without panic, in nights that finally felt like rest,

...in realizing I didn't have to explain myself anymore.

You became the new dream. You're the house I'm building now, one made of truth and stillness, not promises and fear. I promise to keep choosing you, even when chaos calls me back. I promise to protect you the way I once protected everyone else.

And when love finds me again, in this life or the next, I hope it looks a lot like you.

Love,

Fatima Anne

The Renewal Letter

Write a letter beginning with:

"Dear Dream, I thought you left when he did. But I see now you were only waiting for me to come home."

Let it pour out; the grief, the gratitude, the growth.
Seal it, keep it, or burn it as a ritual of release.

The Promise of Peace

You don't have to hate or leave him to move on.

You don't have to burn the past to light the future.

You can love what was, release what isn't, and still bloom right where the dream changed.

Because the story may never have been just about us.

It might have been about you learning that your peace was a part of the dream all along.

Reflection Worksheet:
Grieving the Dream

When the version of love you prayed for changes shape.

What was the original dream you had for this love, this life, or this chapter? (Describe it in vivid detail; how it looked, felt, smelled, sounded.)

____

____

____

____

____

____

____

____

____

____

____

____

When did you first realize the dream was changing? (What moment made you stop pretending everything was fine?)

____

____

____

____

____

____

What part of you is still holding on to that old vision? (Be honest is it the woman who believed, the wife who hoped, or the child who needed safety?)

____

____

____

____

How does disappointment feel in your body? Where does it sit, chest, stomach, throat, etc? What does it sound like?

____

____

____

____

What are you afraid to admit about your grief? (Ex: "I'm mad at God." "I feel stupid for believing." "I miss who he was.")

____

____

____

____

If your grief could speak directly to you, what would it say? Write a letter from your grief to yourself.

____

____

____

____

____

____

____

____

____

____

____

____

____

What did this dream teach you about yourself, your capacity to love, to endure, to create?

____

____

____

What parts of the dream are worth keeping? (Traditions, values, lessons, memories; not everything has to die.)

____

____

____

What new truth did this loss reveal to you about love, partnership, or purpose?

____

____

____

What do you need to forgive yourself for?

____

____

____

____

____

What boundaries or beliefs will protect the next version of your peace?

Write a short goodbye letter to the version of you who was holding the dream together. End it with: "You did your best. You can rest now."

When you picture your life beyond this dream, what small details give you hope?

————————————————————————————

————————————————————————————

————————————————————————————

————————————————————————————

————————————————————————————

————————————————————————————

What does peace look like for you now, in love, in solitude,
in faith?

————————————————————————————

————————————————————————————

————————————————————————————

————————————————————————————

————————————————————————————

————————————————————————————

————————————————————————————

Write one new affirmation that will guide you through this
next chapter: "Even when dreams change, I am still
becoming who I was meant to be."

————————————————————————————

————————————————————————————

Closing Reflection

Light a candle, play your softest song, and reread what you
wrote. Whisper this out loud: "I release the story I wrote for
us. I'm grateful for the chapters we finished. I trust the
author for what comes next."

Fatima's "My Release" Version

I've stopped waiting for what we were supposed to be.

I honor the dream we built, even if it never stood tall.

I no longer carry the blueprint of promises we outgrew.

I grieve what could have been, but I bless what was.

Because even disappointment can be holy when it wakes you up.

I'm not bitter. I'm better. I'm free.

I'm still capable of believing again, just wiser now.

Love,
Fatima Anne

Your Release

What are you letting go of? What are you still learning to forgive? What are you keeping from this experience? What's your goodbye statement?

____

____

____

____

____

____

____

____

____

____

____

____

____

____

____

"Release is not loss, it's redirection."

Staying for Clarity

What Love Looks Like Complicated

PART TWO

Observation. Awareness. Truth.

"Not everything needs a reaction.
Some things need to be seen clearly."

The Decision to Stay (Again)

"Sometimes staying isn't weakness, it's research."

There's a strange kind of silence that comes after you decide not to leave. Not the kind that follows a slammed door or an argument, but the softer one. The silence that hums between two people still sitting in the same house, breathing the same air, but living in two separate timelines. It's the quiet that asks: "Am I still here because I love you, or because I'm afraid to start over?"

I've asked myself that question more times than I care to admit. Each time, I said I was staying to "see things through," but what I really meant was I needed to make sure I'm not crazy. I needed clarity. Not closure. I wanted to see if love could still find us in the same room.

The Unspoken Truth

There's a kind of strength that looks like surrender. It's the moment you stop trying to fix it, stop trying to force it, stop performing for it. You sit in your stillness and say, "I'll stay, but this time I'm watching."

You're not staying to be chosen. You're staying to observe what's true when you stop chasing peace and let the truth reveal itself. You're staying because part of you needs to see if love can survive without you holding it up by yourself. Sometimes staying is the last resort before freedom.

Silence as Data

"Every pause tells a story if you stop trying to fill it."

There comes a point where words stop helping. You've already said everything, the same feelings in a hundred different ways, and somehow, the silence that follows feels louder than all the yelling combined. It's not that he stopped listening. It's that you've both stopped translating. He's speaking survival, you're speaking connection. And neither language fits anymore. So now, you're left studying the pauses.

The Science of Quiet

When love grows uncertain, silence becomes the experiment. What happens when you stop explaining yourself? What happens when you stop initiating the conversation, the cuddle, the compromise? You start to notice how much of the relationship ran on your energy. How much of the peace depended on your planning? How many of the apologies came from your mouth first? Silence shows you who panics when peace is broken and who only shows up when you break it.

The Emotional Math

You begin collecting small data points like a scientist in your own heartbreak:

- Who initiates touch when the day ends?
- Who asks "Are you okay?" first?
- Who sits beside the other in silence, not because they're angry, but because they're still choosing presence?

Silence becomes your truth serum. Every unspoken moment whispers, "This is what love looks like without your effort propping it up. It's uncomfortable, but it's honest.

REFLECTION PROMPTS FOR THE READER:

What has the silence in my home been trying to tell me lately?

____

____

____

When I stop speaking first, who shows up?

____

____

____

What emotions am I afraid to face if I stop filling the silence?

____

____

____

What's the difference between peace and avoidance in my relationship?

____

____

____

Affirmation

"I will not chase clarity through noise. I will let silence reveal the truth. I trust what stays when I stop talking."

Between Obligation and Love

"When the weight of duty starts to look like devotion."

There's a version of love that's built entirely out of promises; the vows, the children, the bills, the memories, the whispered: "we'll figure it out." It's the kind of love that survives not because it's thriving, but because it's rooted in responsibility.

You look around the home you've built and realize: you've become the caretaker of a history, not the participant of a present. Sometimes you stay because you said you would. Sometimes you stay because you can't stand the thought of starting over again, explaining your heart to a new stranger who might still end up disappointing you. Sometimes you stay because it's easier to say "we're fine" than to explain why you're not.

The Invisible Contract

Obligation is a quiet thief. It steals time and disguises itself as loyalty. It tells you that leaving would make you selfish, even when staying has made you small.

You start doing the math:

- How would this affect the kids?
- Who gets the house?
- Who gets the peace?

The truth is, you're not choosing between love and loneliness; you're choosing between comfort and authenticity. You're choosing whether peace should be earned or embodied. Obligation whispers, "Be grateful you have someone." Love whispers, "You deserve to be understood." And sometimes, they sound so similar you can't tell which one is speaking anymore.

The Heart's Confession

When I catch myself saying "we've been through too much to give up now," I ask myself, are we still growing through it, or just enduring it? Because endurance isn't the same as intimacy. Sacrifice isn't the same as love. And longevity isn't proof of joy, it's just proof of time.

Maybe this chapter isn't about choosing whether to stay or go. Maybe it's about recognizing the difference between holding space for love to return, and holding your breath while waiting for it to.

REFLECTION PROMPTS FOR THE READER:

Am I staying because of love or because of guilt?

____

____

What fears surface when I imagine life beyond this relationship?

____

____

____

What does "being loyal" cost me emotionally?

____

____

____

What would staying look like if I were choosing it freely, not fearfully?

____

____

Affirmation

"I can honor my commitments without betraying myself. I release the guilt that confuses love with obligation. I deserve a love that feels chosen, not required."

When Effort Isn't Equal

"When one person keeps showing up while the other keeps showing up late."

There's a moment in every long relationship when you realize you're not fighting each other anymore, you're fighting the imbalance. The weight of who tries harder, who apologizes first, who wants more.

And the most painful part isn't even the effort itself, it's the silence that follows it. The way your partner doesn't seem to notice the thousand invisible things you do just to keep the love from slipping completely off the edge. You start tracking, not because you're petty, but because you're tired.

The Invisible Labor of Love

You remember when effort used to feel mutual, when laughter came easily, when he asked how your day was, when you both cared about making each other's world lighter. Now it feels like you're carrying a love that forgot how to carry you back.

You plan date nights. He scrolls through sports highlights. You initiate deep talks. He says, "Can we not do this right now?" You apologize to keep the peace. He accepts, but never reflects.

This is what unequal effort sounds like: the clink of dishes washed by one person, the quiet of a couch shared by two bodies but no energy, the hollow "thanks" that replaces affection.

The truth is, one person can't keep a relationship breathing on CPR alone.

The Emotional Audit

Sometimes clarity looks like keeping score, not out of spite, but out of self-honesty.

You start asking yourself questions like:

- "When's the last time he initiated a connection?"
- "When's the last time I felt pursued?"
- "When's the last time my needs were met without me having to beg for them?"

You don't track these moments to punish him. You track them to wake yourself up. You can't heal what you refuse to measure. And once you see the pattern, the cancellations, the excuses, the one-sided compromises, you can't unsee it.

The Turning Point

Here's the hardest truth: love doesn't die because people stop feeling. It dies because people stop trying. Effort is the language love speaks when words lose power. Without it, everything else becomes noise, apologies, gifts, even promises.

So maybe this chapter isn't about blaming him for giving less. Maybe it's about asking yourself why you keep accepting imbalance as loyalty. Because sometimes staying isn't strength, it's survival dressed as patience.

REFLECTION PROMPTS FOR THE READER:

What am I doing in this relationship that no one notices but me?

____

____

____

How do I define "trying" in love, and am I the only one doing it?

____

____

____

What do I fear will happen if I stop over-functioning?

____

____

____

What would equal effort feel like in my body?

____

____

____

Affirmation

"I am no longer carrying love by myself. I release the weight of proving my worth through effort. The love meant for me will match my energy, not drain it."

Data Over Drama

"I stopped arguing and started observing."

There's a version of clarity that only comes after you stop explaining yourself. Not because you've given up, but because you've grown tired of hearing your pain turned into proof that you're "doing too much." So, one day, instead of reacting, you start collecting. Not feelings, but facts.

How often does he ask about your day? How often does he listen without checking his phone? How many times has he promised change that never arrived? You become the quiet scientist of your own heartbreak.

The Emotional Spreadsheet

Drama thrives in confusion. It thrives in that fog where love and manipulation sound the same. But the data? Data clears the fog. Data doesn't lie, doesn't gaslight, doesn't need closure.

When you document what's real, the effort, the tone, the timing, you begin to see patterns. You notice which days he's gentle and which days he's absent. You recognize that your sadness spikes after his dismissiveness, not before. You track your own energy, how much light you lose each time you overextend.

This isn't an obsession; it's observation. It's how you reclaim power when you're tired of guessing.

The Clarity Practice

Start a small notebook or a "Truth Log." Each week, record three simple things:

- What I did.
- What he did.
- How it made me feel.

You'll see the trends soon enough. Love that's real is consistent, not conditional. And you'll begin to trust your memory again, not the version he tells you happened, but the version your body remembers. Because your body never forgets when it's been dismissed.

The Reframe

This is what Staying for Clarity really means: You're not waiting for him to change; you're waiting to see the truth clearly enough to decide for yourself. You stop defending your emotions. You stop arguing your case. You realize your clarity doesn't need his cooperation. When you know what you know, the drama loses its audience.

REFLECTION PROMPTS FOR THE READER:

What patterns have I noticed when I stop reacting and just observe?

____

____

How does my body respond to peace vs. confusion?

____

____

____

What evidence do I already have that something has shifted between us?

____

____

____

What truths am I afraid to admit because it might mean the story is ending?

____

____

____

Affirmation

"I don't chase closure anymore, I collect clarity. I no longer need an argument to validate my truth. My peace is found in what's proven, not promised."

The Edge of Intimacy

"Our bodies remember even when our hearts forget."

There's a moment when touches change. When what used to feel like connection begins to feel like choreography, the motions are familiar, but the meaning's missing. You still lie beside each other, but it feels like a performance no one's watching anymore.

The body keeps trying to reach where the heart used to live, and all it finds is distance.

The Space Between Us

At first, you think it's stress. He's tired, you're busy, life happens. But one day, you realize the problem isn't timing, it's presence.

The kisses are shorter. The hugs last just long enough to keep up appearances. The "I love you" sounds more like punctuation than promises.

You start to miss what used to come naturally, not just the sex, but the laughter between it. The closeness that didn't have to be earned. The casual brush of a hand that said, "I still see you." Now, everything feels like permission you have to give. And somehow, you're both starving in a house full of food.

The Quiet Hunger

Intimacy isn't just physical; it's emotional vulnerability made visible. When that breaks, the body feels lonely even in company. You start overthinking every gesture, every pause, every sigh. You miss him, even when he's right beside you. You wonder if he misses you too, or just the version of you that required less effort.

The hardest part isn't that the intimacy faded, it's realizing how long you've been pretending it didn't.

REFLECTION PROMPTS FOR THE READER:

What moments made me realize our intimacy was shifting?

____

____

____

Do I still crave closeness with him, or just the idea of what we used to have?

____

____

____

What does my body need from love right now: safety, passion, or honesty?

____

____

How can I reconnect to myself without waiting for him to show up first?

____

____

____

Affirmation

"I honor my body's truth. I will not confuse proximity with connection. I deserve to be touched with intention, not obligation."

What the Mirror Keeps Showing

"I kept trying to fix him, but really, I was trying to save the version of me who thought she could."

There's a point in every season of staying where you start to see yourself clearly. Not the version of you that shows up for others, but the one that sits alone at night, wondering how she got here again. It's not self-blame; it's self-awareness. Because somewhere between loving him and losing yourself, you stopped noticing how much of your identity became tied to how well you were doing together.

The Reflection You Avoid

Sometimes the hardest thing to look at isn't the person who disappointed you, it's the person you became while trying to love them. You used to laugh louder. Dream bigger. Move freer. Now, you shrink your tone, schedule your emotions, and pray that softness won't be mistaken for weakness.

The mirror doesn't lie. It shows you the fatigue in your eyes, the tension in your jaw, the glow that used to mean joy but now just means survival. And the scariest part? You've gotten so used to it that you call it normal. But the mirror doesn't judge, it just asks, "Do you still recognize yourself here?"

The Myth of Martyrdom

We grow up believing that strength means enduring everything. That love that lasts is love that sacrifices. That being the bigger person means being the quieter one. But that belief builds martyrs, not partners. And you, my love, are not here to die for connection. You're here to live inside it, with voice, with agency, with boundaries that love can bounce safely between.

The mirror keeps showing you where you overfunction. Where you mother the man instead of meeting him. Where you take silence as an invitation to over-explain. You confuse loyalty with self-abandonment. These patterns aren't proof of weakness; they're proof of wiring. You were taught that keeping the peace was more important than keeping yourself. But peace built on suppression is just exhaustion in disguise.

The Work of Returning

Clarity isn't about changing him, it's about coming home to you. Because once you see yourself again, you will stop negotiating your worth. You will stop calling your own needs "too much." You stop mistaking gratitude for grace when it's really guilt. Look closer. You are not the problem, you're the pattern-breaker. You're the one who decided to turn pain into perspective. And that, beloved, is the most honest kind of healing there is.

REFLECTION PROMPTS FOR THE READER:

How do I sound when I'm speaking from peace versus pain?

____

____

____

What conversations am I avoiding because I'm afraid of being misunderstood?

____

____

____

How can I practice calm communication without silencing my truth?

____

____

____

What does my "peace voice" sound like, and what boundaries protect it?

____

____

____

Affirmation

I will speak from my center, not my chaos. My calm is not compliance, it's clarity. I choose words that water, not wounds."

The Language of Peace

"I had to learn that silence and softness aren't the same thing."

Peace has a sound. It's not the absence of conflict; it's the tone you use when you've outgrown fighting for understanding. There was a time when I spoke from my wounds instead of my wisdom. When every conversation turned into an emotional tug-of-war. I was defending, proving, performing, trying to convince a man who had already made peace with not hearing me. But peace doesn't live in persuasion. Peace lives in presence.

The Power of Tone

You can say "I'm tired" in five different ways, and each one tells a different story.

One says I'm angry.
One says I'm hopeless.
One says I'm warning you before I break.
And one says I'm ready to try, but I need help.

Tone is how your soul leaks through your words. And when your tone changes, your entire home changes with it. I started asking myself before speaking: "Am I saying this to be heard, or to be right?"

That question saved me from so many circular arguments. It reminded me that peace isn't passive,it's precision.

The 24-Hour Rule

Not everything deserves an immediate reaction. Some things just need distance. When I started giving my emotions a day to breathe before responding, I realized how many of my "urgent" arguments weren't really urgent, they were just reactions to my own disappointment. Waiting gave me perspective. It gave me language that didn't hurt. It gave me ownership of my peace instead of handing it to his mood swings.

The New Dialogue

Peaceful communication doesn't mean silence; it means strategy.

Instead of saying: "You don't listen to me."
 Say: "I feel dismissed when my words don't seem to matter."

Instead of: "You never do anything romantic."
 Say: "I miss feeling pursued by you.

"Instead of: "You make me feel crazy."
Say: "This situation confuses my emotions, can we slow down?"

This is not softness for his comfort. This is softness for your sanity. Because the goal isn't to win. It's to stay whole.

REFLECTION PROMPTS FOR THE READER:

What part of myself have I silenced in order to keep the peace?

____

____

____

How have I overfunctioned in this relationship?

____

____

____

What story does my reflection tell, and what story do I want to rewrite?

____

____

____

What boundaries would honor the version of me I'm becoming?

____

____

____

Affirmation

"I will no longer edit myself to be loved. The woman in the mirror is worth the full truth, even when it's uncomfortable. I forgive who I was when I didn't know better."

The Cost of Clarity

"The truth freed me, but first it broke me."

Clarity doesn't always come with calm. Sometimes it arrives like an earthquake, shaking every foundation you built just to prove which ones were never solid. You pray for the truth, but you forget that truth doesn't show up dressed in comfort. It walks in wearing confrontation, carrying grief in one hand and relief in the other. It doesn't whisper, it wrecks. And yet, even in that wreckage, there's something sacred.

The Breaking Point

You thought clarity would feel like peace. Instead, it feels like a clean wound, no infection, but plenty of pain. It's the night you stop blaming miscommunication and start accepting misalignment. It's the moment you stop asking, "Why won't he love me right?" and start accepting, "Maybe he can't."

You realize he's not withholding effort out of malice; he's just at capacity. And you? You've been living on emotional credit, overdrafting your soul trying to sustain a love that doesn't deposit back. That realization hurts more than the fights ever did. Because fights meant there was still fire. Clarity means the fire's out.

The Emotional Invoice

Every truth has a price. You pay in tears, in silence, in the collapse of the fantasy you kept on life support. You grieve the version of him you kept believing in. You grieve the future you narrated in your head. You grieve the woman who kept trying to prove she was worth consistency. But the beauty of grief is that it's proof of value, you only mourn what mattered. And maybe that's how clarity repays you: by showing you what was real, even if it didn't last.

The Rebuild

Clarity clears space. You stop begging for closure from the same person who broke the peace. You stop writing apologies you don't owe. You start realizing you've been speaking fluent forgiveness in a place that stopped deserving it.

And here's the secret nobody tells you, once clarity lands, you can never un-know it. You can't go back to pretending. You can't unknow how empty "we're fine" feels. You can only decide how to move forward, broken but honest, bruised but awake.

REFLECTION PROMPTS FOR THE READER:

What truth have I been avoiding because I fear its consequences?

———————————————————————————

———————————————————————————

———————————————————————————

How have I been paying for peace that never arrives?

———————————————————————————

———————————————————————————

———————————————————————————

What version of the relationship am I finally ready to release?

———————————————————————————

———————————————————————————

———————————————————————————

How can I honor my pain without becoming loyal to it?

———————————————————————————

———————————————————————————

Affirmation

Clarity may have cost me comfort, but it bought me peace. I no longer confuse pain with passion or chaos with care. I am free, even if I'm still healing.

If I Stay, Let It Be Different

"If I'm going to stay, I refuse to stay the same."

There comes a moment when staying no longer means settling; it just means restructuring. When love stops being something you chase and starts being something you negotiate. You're not the same woman who entered this relationship. You've survived silence, imbalance, disappointment, and clarity. You've grown an emotional backbone made of both softness and boundaries. And now, if you stay, it won't be out of habit. It will be out of choice.

The New Terms of Love

The truth is: staying only makes sense if the structure changes. You can't pour new energy into an old system. If peace doesn't live here yet, it has to be invited, not begged for.

You start redefining what partnership looks like:

- No more being the default emotional manager.
- No more conversations that end with confusion instead of compromise.
- No more calling your boundaries "attitude."

If I stay, let there be new rules. Rules where silence doesn't replace intimacy. Where accountability isn't optional. Where the apology is matched by an adjustment.

The Power of Conditions

Love can be unconditional, but access to you shouldn't be. If he wants to stay, too, then both of you have to decide what "different" means in practice.

Ask the hard questions:

- How do we repair trust, not just promise it?
- How do we schedule time for us again, not as a chore, but a ritual?
- How do we measure effort beyond words?

This is where love meets logistics. Healing doesn't happen through "we'll see." It happens through intentional redesign. Because love without structure eventually collapses under its own hope.

The Personal Shift

This is the chapter where you turn the focus inward again. If I stay, let me stay honest. If I stay, let me stay open, but not unguarded. If I stay, let me stop pretending to be "fine."

If he never changes, I can still change how I respond. If he never meets me halfway, I can still walk my half with peace. If he chooses complacency, I choose clarity, and that choice will never be wasted. Because sometimes staying isn't about keeping the relationship alive, it's about keeping yourself alive inside the relationship.

REFLECTION PROMPTS FOR THE READER:

What conditions must be present for staying to feel peaceful, not punishing?

____

____

____

What patterns am I no longer willing to participate in?

____

____

____

What actions (not words) would show me that change is possible?

____

____

____

How can I practice self-respect daily, even if love still feels uncertain?

____

____

Affirmation

"If I stay, it will be as a woman reborn. I am no longer available for cycles that drain me. Love will meet me at my healed frequency or it will pass me by."

Preparing for Either Outcome

Clarity doesn't always lead to endings. Sometimes it leads to options. The woman you are now, the one who's done the emotional math, who stopped performing, who knows the cost, she can no longer live on "maybe." You're not choosing to stay or leave right now. You're choosing to be ready. Ready if it works. Ready if it doesn't. Ready to stop breaking every time love shifts shape.

The Emotional Exit Plan

Even if you never walk away, you need to know that you could. There's peace in knowing that your survival doesn't depend on his participation. That if love walks out, you won't crumble, you'll recalibrate.

Start small:

- Know where you'd go for peace, even if it's just your best friend's couch or your mama's kitchen.
- Know your money, where it lives, and what it owes you.
- Know what you need emotionally to function. What fills your cup when no one else pours.

Preparation doesn't mean you're planning to leave. It means you're refusing to be trapped.

The Internal Readiness

Emotional preparedness isn't cold. It's clarity with compassion. Ask yourself: "What would peace look like if I stayed?" "What would healing look like if I left?"

Neither answer should terrify you because either way, peace should follow you. You're building an inner ecosystem that doesn't collapse depending on the outcome. You stop seeing the relationship as a life sentence. It becomes a lesson, a choice, a living thing that must be fed or released.

The Art of Emotional Detachment

Detachment doesn't mean apathy. It means protection with softness. You learn to love him without losing yourself. To listen without absorbing. To care without clinging. You become the observer again; calm, grounded, unattached to outcomes. Because when you're no longer addicted to reassurance, you start living from power instead of panic. This is what emotional maturity looks like. You can still love someone deeply and still choose yourself if it stops being safe to stay.

REFLECTION PROMPTS FOR THE READER:

What would I need (financially, emotionally, spiritually) to feel safe either way?

____

____

____

What does readiness look like for me, practically and energetically?

____

____

How can I prepare my heart without hardening it?

____

____

____

What does peace require from me regardless of his behavior?

____

____

____

Affirmation

"I am no longer afraid of endings. I prepare for peace, not panic. Whether I stay or go, I will land on my feet, steady, sacred, and sure."

Staying for Myself

"Even if nothing changes, I can."

There's a kind of peace that doesn't require agreement. It's not loud or dramatic. It doesn't arrive with grand gestures or perfect timing. It comes quietly with the decision to keep becoming yourself, no matter who notices.

That's what staying for yourself looks like. It's staying present, not stuck. It's staying aware, not angry. It's staying in love with your life even if the relationship doesn't mirror that love back yet.

The Reclamation

You used to think that self-love and marriage couldn't coexist. That choosing yourself somehow meant betraying him. But now you understand that love isn't subtraction; it's stewardship. You can tend to your peace while still being in the same house.

You stop waiting for him to lead your healing and start leading yourself through it. You start filling your mornings with purpose again: the gym, your journaling, your music, your breath. You make plans that feed your soul instead of waiting for his schedule to open.

You begin to realize: staying doesn't have to mean shrinking. It can mean stabilizing until your spirit says otherwise.

The New Identity

This version of you isn't performing wifehood anymore. She's practicing wholeness. She doesn't beg for attention; she cultivates it from within. She doesn't fight for space; she occupies it. You don't have to end the relationship to outgrow its old dynamics. Sometimes growth itself ends the version of love that can no longer hold you. And that's okay. That's sacred. That's clarity fulfilled.

The Everyday Practice

To stay for yourself means creating rituals that restore your peace daily:

- Morning gratitude before any conversation.
- Breathing before reacting.
- Journaling before texting.
- Resting without guilt.
- Choosing beauty, flowers, candles, laughter, even if no one else joins you.

Because your joy isn't rebellion; it's reclamation. And one day, if he ever asks what changed, you can smile softly and say: "I did."

REFLECTION PROMPTS FOR THE READER:

What does staying for myself mean in my daily life?

____

____

____

How can I keep growing even if my partner doesn't?

____

____

____

What does peace look like inside my body right now?

____

____

____

How can I celebrate my healing while still navigating love's complexity?

____

____

____

Affirmation

"I am no longer waiting for someone to make me whole. I am already complete. Whether this love rises with me or fades behind me, I will keep choosing myself, over and over again."

INTERLUDE:

Peace didn't arrive with fireworks.
It came while I was making breakfast.
No grand moment.
No announcement.
Just quiet.
Just life... finally mine again.
The ordinary became sacred.
Not because life changed... but because I did.

Between Promise & Peace

Staying Steady Through Uncertainity

PART THREE

Release. Identity. Self-Return.

"Peace didn't ask me to let go of love.
It taught me how to hold myself first."

The Quiet After the Storm

"Silence hits different when it's no longer heavy."

After the heartbreak, there's a silence that isn't sadness, it's space. The kind of quiet that feels earned. No yelling, no tension, no waiting for the other shoe to drop. Just the soft hum of your own breathing, steady and sovereign. For the first time in a long time, peace doesn't scare you. You're not afraid of your own company. You're not sprinting toward distraction. You're just... still.

The Unfamiliar Calm

It's strange at first, this stillness. You spent years, damn near your whole life, living in survival mode, measuring safety by someone else's moods. Now, there's no chaos to decode, no apologies to hope for, no arguments rehearsed in your head. You realize how loud love has gotten. You noticed how much emotional noise you tolerated to feel less alone. Now, you wake up to the sound of birds outside your window, the smell of your own tea, and the sound of your kids laughing in the next room. Life didn't end, it just got quieter. And maybe that's the miracle, realizing that peace was never gone, just buried under the noise.

The Emotional Detox

Peace feels awkward when you're used to pain. You'll catch yourself waiting for conflict to return. You'll miss the adrenaline that came from fixing, explaining, and overextending. But don't confuse boredom with healing. Stillness is the body's way of recovering from years of over-functioning. Let yourself rest. Let the calm feel foreign. You're detoxing from emotional chaos; it's going to feel strange before it feels sacred.

The Spiritual Reset

The storm stripped away illusions, not identity. You are still capable of deep love, deep joy, deep purpose, but now you give it from overflow, not emptiness. This is where the rebuilding begins. You start talking to God again (whoever that may be to you). You're not begging, but just breathing. You start moving your body for strength, not revenge. You start remembering the parts of you that existed before disappointment taught you to shrink.

This chapter of your life isn't about proving you're healed. It's about becoming safe inside your own skin again.

REFLECTION PROMPTS FOR THE READER:

How do I feel when the world is finally quiet around me?

____

____

____

What old habits try to pull me back into chaos?

____

____

____

What small rituals help me feel grounded in peace?

____

____

____

How can I honor my healing without rushing it?

____

____

____

Affirmation

"I am no longer afraid of quiet. Stillness does not mean emptiness; it means alignment. I survived the storm. Now I deserve the calm."

The Detox of False Hope

"I kept believing he'd come back different, not realizing I never left the same."

Hope can be addictive. You tell yourself it's faith. You call it patience. You wrap it in love and label it loyalty. But sometimes, hope becomes the prettiest form of self-abandonment. You start waiting for change instead of creating it. You start calling disappointment "almost." You start mistaking time for progress. And when that hope doesn't deliver, it doesn't just break your heart; it bruises your self-trust.

The Illusion of "Maybe"

"Maybe he'll grow up."
 "Maybe he'll see what he's losing."
"Maybe he'll love me the way I love him."

The word "maybe" becomes a leash. It keeps you in emotional limbo, not moving forward, but not letting go. You start curating your life around his potential. You measure your joy in small crumbs of improvement, a kinder tone here, sweet gestures here and there, but the foundation never changes.

You begin to realize: you were more in love with the version of him that lived in your head than the one who stood in front of you. That's not foolishness. That's faith misplaced. You believed in love the way it should be, and there's no shame in that. But healing means calling "hope" what it really was, a habit.

The Withdrawal

Letting go of false hope feels like breaking an emotional addiction. You'll crave the dopamine of potential. You'll want to check his social media, reread old texts, and imagine him finally getting it. But detox means choosing reality, even when it's duller than the dream. It's learning to be okay with the idea that he might never "come back right." That he might never apologize the way you need him to. And that's not tragedy, that's the truth. You're not losing your person. You're losing the illusion that kept you small.

The Healing Reframe

Detoxing from false hope doesn't mean you stop believing in love; it means you start believing in your discernment. You realize that hope without accountability is just denial in a prettier dress. You stop rooting for potential and start choosing reciprocity. You stop romanticizing the version of him that existed only in your memory. Because peace doesn't come from fixing someone else, it comes from trusting yourself to stop trying.

REFLECTION PROMPTS FOR THE READER:

What versions of him (or us) am I still waiting to see again?

____

____

How does my body react when I choose hope over honesty?

____

____

What would letting go of "maybe" free me to do right now?

____

____

How can I start building a life that doesn't hinge on his evolution?

____

____

____

Affirmation

"I release the version of love I imagined. I honor what was real, and I grieve what was fantasy. My hope now belongs to my healing."

Unlearning Survival

"My body kept fighting long after the war was over."

Healing didn't start with peace; it started with confusion. You weren't sure who you were without the constant alertness. You'd built an entire identity around endurance, showing up, fixing things, making do. And when the chaos finally stopped, your nervous system didn't believe it. Your body was still waiting for the next apology, the next explosion, the next shift in tone. That's the cruelty of survival mode; even when the threat leaves, it keeps living inside you.

The Body Remembers

You notice it in the little things:

- The way your shoulders tense when someone raises their voice.
- The way you over-explain simple truths, afraid they'll be twisted.
- The way you can't fully rest because rest feels like weakness.

Your body doesn't know the storm is over yet. It still thinks peace is the setup before the fall. So it stays alert. Hypervigilant. Guarded. But now, your work isn't to fight. It's to teach your body that peace is safe again.

Rewiring the Reflex

You start small. A deep breath before reacting. A walk without your phone. Saying "no" and not explaining why. Letting someone else handle something, even if they don't do it perfectly. Every tiny act of rest is rebellion against the version of you that thought survival was your only option.

You remind yourself:

"Nothing bad happens when I rest."
"I don't have to earn calm."
"Peace is not the pause before pain."

That's the reprogramming, not forcing yourself to be fearless, but learning to stop waiting for the storm.

Reclaiming Safety

Safety isn't a place; it's a relationship with your own nervous system. It's when your heart rate slows down during silence. When you stop translating every sigh into rejection. When you stop expecting punishment for peace. You stop scanning for danger and start scanning for joy. You notice the smell of your favorite candle. The warmth of sunlight through the blinds. The small victory of waking up without dread. That's what unlearning survival looks like: peace in the body, not just in the mind.

REFLECTION PROMPTS FOR THE READER:

What behaviors do I still carry from survival mode?

____

____

____

What triggers make me feel unsafe even when I am safe?

____

____

____

How can I show my body that calm is allowed?

____

____

____

What does safety feel like in my body today?

____

____

____

Affirmation

"I am no longer living on high alert. The war is over, even if my body forgets sometimes. I choose rest. I choose ease. I choose peace."

Soft Doesn't Mean Weak

"I learned to put my crown down without ever putting my power away."

There's a kind of woman the world misreads, the one who can cry and still conquer. The one who prays, but also pays bills. The one who shows grace, even to those who never deserved her gentleness. That woman is you. And for a long time, you confused softness with weakness because every time you let your guard down, someone mishandled it. But this time, softness isn't a risk. It's a rebellion.

The Armor You Outgrew

You built walls that once kept you safe, silent, sarcastic, and hyper-independent. You told yourself, "I don't need anyone," because needing people hurts. But walls that protect can also imprison. You became the strong one, the reliable one, the backbone, and now your back is tired. Because "strong" was never supposed to be your only identity.

So you start taking the armor off, not all at once, but piece by piece. You breathe deeper. You speak more gently. You forgive slower, but fuller. And you remember that strength doesn't always roar; sometimes it whispers, "I'm done fighting what's meant to flow."

The Return of Soft Power

Softness is not about being quiet; it's about being intentional. It's smiling because you want to, not because you're afraid of conflict. It's choosing love again, but with boundaries sharp enough to draw blood if crossed. Softness is grace with a backbone. It's the ability to nurture and still say "no." To be kind without being compliant. To care without being consumed. You learn that femininity isn't fragility, it's frequency. And you, beloved, are finally tuned back to peace.

The Reframe

The world taught you to protect your heart like a weapon. But now, you're learning to protect it like a garden. You plant forgiveness, not for him, but for your future. You water your joy with time, not approval. And you prune away everything that doesn't grow with you. This isn't a retreat from power, it's a return to authenticity. Because the most powerful thing a healed woman can do is stop performing pain.

REFLECTION PROMPTS FOR THE READER:

What does "soft" look like for me when it's safe?

____

____

____

What armor have I outgrown?

____

____

____

How can I honor both my boundaries and my tenderness?

____

____

____

Who taught me that being gentle meant being powerless, and do I still believe them?

____

____

____

Affirmation

"My softness is not a flaw, it's my freedom. I can be gentle and grounded, tender and true. I am power in its most peaceful form."

Touching Yourself Back to Life

"My body stopped waiting for permission to feel good again."

Healing isn't just emotional, it's physical. After years of shrinking to survive, your body forgets what safety feels like. You learn to go numb, not because you want to, but because you had to. So when peace finally comes, it doesn't feel natural; it feels like a stranger knocking at your skin. This chapter is about opening that door again.

The Return to Sensation

You spent so long reading someone else's body language that you forgot how to listen to your own. You knew how to soothe him, how to comfort everyone else, but when it came to yourself, touch became mechanical.

Now, you begin reintroducing intimacy, not as performance, but as presence. You run your hands over your arms and remember what softness feels like. You moisturize your skin like it deserves attention, not correction. You stretch and breathe like you're worshiping the body that carried you through chaos. It's not about sex, it's about aliveness. It's about realizing that your body doesn't need validation to be sacred.

The Mirror Work

For so long, you looked at your reflection like a report card. Criticizing your stomach, your stretch marks, your exhaustion. Now you start looking like a witness instead of a judge. You see the woman who endured sleepless nights and still woke up to nurture, grind, and give. You see the resilience in your thighs, the grace in your hands, the softness that refused to disappear.

You whisper to her:

"Thank you for staying."
"You're safe now."
"You're still beautiful."

And one day, it won't feel awkward to say it. It'll feel like the truth returning home.

The Divine Feminine Frequency

Your sensuality is your birthright, not a gift someone gives to you.

You begin reconnecting with it through gentle rituals:

- Dancing alone in your kitchen.
- Lighting a candle just because you like the scent.

- Wearing perfume even when no one's around.
- Playing music that makes your hips remember joy.

You're not trying to become sexy again because you're realizing you never stopped being it. You just stopped prioritizing it. Your sensual energy isn't about seduction; it's about creation. It's what builds art, babies, business, and balance. It's the quiet hum of womanhood restored.

REFLECTION PROMPTS FOR THE READER:

How have I disconnected from my own body during survival?

____

____

____

What rituals make me feel at home in my skin again?

____

____

____

How can I practice intimacy with myself that isn't sexual, but sacred?

____

____

____

What parts of me am I ready to see as beautiful again?

____

____

____

Affirmation

"I am safe in my body. My softness is divine, my skin is sacred. I do not need permission to feel good again, I am the permission."

Forgiveness Without Return

"I forgave him the moment I realized he could never repay the debt."

Forgiveness isn't always a conversation. Sometimes it's a quiet decision you make alone. The kind that doesn't need his apology or your explanation. Because forgiveness isn't about him anymore. It's about freeing you from the version of yourself that stayed too long in emotional captivity.

The Myth of Closure

We grow up believing closure is a two-person job. That healing requires both sides to sit down, talk, and agree on what went wrong. But sometimes, the people who hurt you don't have the capacity, courage, or consciousness to see it. You could write a thesis on the pain they caused, and they'd still tell you you're overreacting. You could wait for years for the apology that never comes, and in the meantime, you'd still be living under their emotional jurisdiction. So you stop waiting for them to wake up. You wake up for yourself. Forgiveness, in this season, isn't reconciliation. It's a reclamation.

The Emotional Debt

He owes you an acknowledgement. He owes you accountability. He owes you the version of himself he promised to become. But you've stopped doing emotional accounting because waiting for repayment keeps your spirit in overdraft. You realize that every ounce of resentment you carry still ties your energy to him, still keeps you reacting to his absence, still keeps you shaping your healing around his name. So you cancel the debt. Not because it's fair. Because it's freedom.

Forgiveness ≠ Access

Forgiveness doesn't mean open doors, it means open hands. It's choosing to let go, not to let him back in. You can release the story without revisiting the character. You're not healing for reconciliation, you're healing for regulation. For rest. For rhythm. You forgive to stop rehearsing the pain. You forgive to hear your own heartbeat again without the noise of what happened. Forgiveness is your exit strategy.

The Reframe

Forgiveness doesn't erase accountability; it restores balance. You no longer need him to suffer to validate your pain. You've done the work. You've lived through the consequences. Now you get to live without the weight. Forgiveness is not weakness. It's your final act of self-respect. You're no longer defined by what was done to you. You're defined by what you choose to release.

REFLECTION PROMPTS FOR THE READER:

What emotional debts am I still waiting for someone to repay?

____

____

____

How has holding on served me, and how has it kept me stuck?

____

____

____

What boundaries protect my forgiveness from becoming access?

____

____

____

How will I know when I'm free?

____

____

____

Affirmation

"I release the weight of waiting for an apology. I forgive not to reconcile, but to restore my peace. I no longer live in emotional debt; I am free."

There comes a point where you stop searching for safety in other people and start realizing you are supposed to become it for yourself. For years, home meant him. His mood. His presence. His consistency. If he felt close, you relaxed. If he pulled away, your nervous system followed him into uncertainty. You built your sense of peace around someone else's emotional availability, and that kind of love will exhaust you every time.

So now, you begin again. Not by abandoning love, but by rebuilding the relationship you have with yourself.

Building a Home Within

"I stopped waiting for someone to build with me and started building myself."

Peace becomes different once you stop treating it like something another person gives you. You realize safety is not found in promises, apologies, or temporary closeness. It's built slowly. Intentionally. Through boundaries, self-trust, routine, and the quiet decision to stop abandoning yourself just because someone else does.

This is the chapter where healing becomes practical.

Becoming the Safe Place

You spent years trying to be everyone else's safe space. The calm one. The understanding one. The emotionally responsible one. You soothed arguments, carried conversations, softened tension, and cleaned up emotional messes that were never yours alone to hold.

And while you were busy being safety for everyone else, you forgot to create any for yourself.

Now, you begin asking different questions:

What makes me feel safe in my own body?
What drains my nervous system?
What boundaries protect my peace instead of punishing my honesty?

You begin to realize peace is not a person. It's a practice. You stop depending on someone else's consistency to feel emotionally stable. You stop handing people the power to determine whether your day feels calm or chaotic.

You become the voice that says:

"You're okay."
"You don't have to panic."
"You're allowed to rest now."

That's not selfishness. That's self-return.

The Emotional Architecture

You start designing your inner world differently.

Your foundation becomes self-trust. You stop second-guessing your intuition every time your spirit tells you something feels off. You stop overriding your own discomfort just to keep the peace.

Your walls become boundaries. Soft ones. Strong ones. Boundaries that allow love in without allowing confusion to take over the entire house.

Your windows become perspective. Gratitude. Openness without self-erasure.

And your roof becomes faith. The quiet understanding that even when life shifts, you will still know how to hold yourself through it.

You are no longer surviving love. You are learning how to sustain yourself within it.

The Financial Safety Net

Healing is emotional, but peace is practical too. Stress settles in places where instability lives. So you stop avoiding your finances and start treating them like part of your healing journey.

You save money not from fear, but from freedom. You create cushions that allow you to breathe easier. You stop seeing independence as rebellion and start seeing it as wisdom. You learn your numbers. You prepare yourself. You build stability that does not depend entirely on another person's choices. Not because you're planning to leave, but because you deserve to feel secure either way. And there's something powerful about knowing your peace has options.

The Daily Sanctuary

You also begin rebuilding yourself through routine. You make your bed because your environment affects your spirit. You light candles because your peace deserves softness. You cook nourishing meals because care should not only exist when someone else offers it to you. You stop treating daily rituals like small things and start understanding they are how healing becomes sustainable.

A quiet morning.
A clean kitchen.
A journal entry before bed.
Music while folding clothes.
Breathing before reacting.

This is how peace enters the body. Repetition. Consistency. Intention. You stop waiting for a dramatic transformation and begin honoring steady restoration instead.

The Inner Rooms

Inside yourself, there are rooms that need care too.

The Room of Rest, where guilt is not allowed to follow you.

The Room of Joy, where laughter still lives without explanation.

The Room of Reflection, where your truth can exist unedited and honest.

The Room of Boundaries, where "no" becomes a complete sentence instead of a negotiation.

And at the center of it all, The Room of Grace, where you forgive yourself for every version of you that stayed too long, tried too hard, or confused survival with love. You stop seeing yourself as broken. You start seeing yourself as under reconstruction.

The Rebuild

Building a home within yourself does not mean you stop loving other people. It means you stop disappearing inside them. You stop asking relationships to provide what only self-trust can sustain. You stop chasing emotional safety from people who are still at war with themselves. And slowly, your life begins to feel different. Softer. Steadier. More honest. Not because everything around you changed overnight, but because you did.

Peace lives in you now. Not perfectly. Not permanently. But intentionally. And that changes everything.

REFLECTION PROMPTS FOR THE READER:

What makes me feel emotionally safe in my daily life?

What routines help me feel grounded and calm?

What boundaries protect my peace instead of restricting my joy?

What parts of myself still need gentleness while I heal?

Affirmation

"I am no longer waiting for someone else to make me feel safe. I am my own foundation, my own sanctuary, and my own home."

Choosing Quiet Over Closure

"I stopped needing the last word to know I was right."

Closure used to mean answers, the talk, the apology, the understanding. But now, you've learned that silence can be an answer too. Sometimes, peace doesn't come from fixing things; it comes from no longer fighting them. You still love him. You still see the pieces that could work. But you've stopped dragging your spirit through the mud, trying to make every piece fit. Quiet isn't giving up. Quiet is alignment.

The Myth of "Finishing the Conversation"

You used to believe that every wound needed a witness, that he had to get it for you to heal from it. But closure isn't comprehension. It's acceptance. And sometimes, the conversations you keep trying to have are only reopening wounds that have already told you what you needed to know. You're realizing that his silence says enough. His patterns are paragraphs. His inconsistency is in communication. You don't need another explanation. You need exhalation. So now, when the tension rises and the words start circling, you choose calm instead of chaos. You let the silence end what the argument couldn't.

The Middle Space of Love

You're still here. Still hoping, still trying, still loving him in the only way you can without losing yourself. But now, you love with boundaries. You speak without begging. You listen without abandoning your peace. You've stopped needing the perfect moment of closure to believe in your healing. You're learning to live in the in-between, the space where you can love someone deeply and still protect your own light. Because peace doesn't mean you stopped caring. It means you stopped chasing.

The Grace of Letting Be

You no longer force growth. You plant seeds and let time decide what blooms. You show up as love, but you don't perform it for points. You give effort without resentment and rest without guilt. You can still share a home and a heart without surrendering your sanity. You can still try without losing your truth. Closure doesn't always mean endings. Sometimes it just means, "I've said enough. I've seen enough. I can stay, but with peace."

REFLECTION PROMPTS FOR THE READER:

What conversations am I still trying to have that no longer serve peace?

____

____

____

What would choosing quiet look like without feeling like defeat?

____

____

____

How can I love him without silencing myself?

____

____

____

What does "peaceful effort" mean in my marriage right now?

____

____

____

Affirmation

"I no longer chase understanding. I can love without explaining, forgive without forgetting, and stay without suffering. I choose quiet because I trust what peace reveals."

When Peace Becomes the Promise

"I stopped promising forever and started promising peace."

Once upon a time, your love story was built on big dreams and beautiful maybes. You talked about what you'd build, where you'd go, what the future would look like, all that promise, bright and blinding. But somewhere along the way, the promise got heavy. It became pressure. It became proof. It became the test you both kept failing. Now, you're rewriting that vow. You're no longer chasing the promise of perfection; you're choosing the promise of peace.

The Shift

Peace used to feel like surrender. Like the thing you got when you stopped caring. But now, you understand it's the highest form of maturity, loving without losing your center, showing up without losing your sense. You no longer fight to be right. You no longer beg to be seen. You no longer need to prove the depth of your effort to feel worthy of calm. Now, peace is the standard. Not the prize.

The New Promise

You and him may not have the story you imagined, but that doesn't mean you can't build one that feels softer, safer, more sustainable.

So you make new vows:

I promise to communicate with care, even when I'm frustrated.

I promise to protect my peace before my pride.

I promise to love myself loud enough to remind him what love sounds like.

I promise to stay if it feels like growth, and to leave if it starts to feel like survival.

These are not wedding vows. They're healing vows. A new covenant with yourself, rooted in peace instead of performance.

The Relearning of Love

When peace becomes the promise, you stop loving from fear; fear of loss, rejection, change, or misunderstanding. You start loving from truth. From acceptance. From a heart that knows: "Even if this doesn't last forever, it still mattered. It still grew me." You no longer measure success by longevity, but by alignment. You no longer chase forever; you chase fulfillment. You love deeply, but lightly. You try, but you rest. You give, but you keep something for yourself too. This is the season of peaceful love.

What Staying Looks Like Now

You're still here; still married, still showing up, still hoping. But your staying has evolved. It's no longer about holding the title of "wife", it's about holding space for yourself. You've redefined love to include peace, and that changes everything. You speak softly, but with boundaries. You forgive, but with awareness. You dream, but without delusion. You don't need the relationship to be perfect to feel whole because your peace is no longer conditional on him. It's the promise you made to yourself.

REFLECTION PROMPTS FOR THE READER:

What promises have I made to myself that protect my peace?

____

____

____

How can I love him and still honor my own evolution?

____

____

____

What does peace look like in motion, not as a word, but as a daily practice?

____

____

____

What does "trying differently" mean for me right now?

____

____

____

Affirmation

"Peace is my new promise. I no longer chase forever; I build balance. I am staying, but differently. My love is no longer a storm, it's a sanctuary."

The Benediction of Becoming

"Peace didn't save me, it revealed who I've always been."

There comes a moment after all the heartbreak, hope, and hard lessons, where you stop trying to "get back" to yourself and realize you've outgrown the old version entirely. You're not returning to who you were before the storm. You're becoming who you were meant to be because of it. Becoming isn't an arrival; it's a rhythm.

It's waking up and choosing alignment over attachment. It's knowing that love can be imperfect and still sacred. It's forgiving without pretending. It's staying, not for the image, not for the obligation, but because peace lives here now, in you.

The Reflection of the Healed

You stand differently now. Your silence is confident, not cautious. Your smile is rooted, not rehearsed. You still care, but it no longer costs you your clarity. You love your husband, but you also love your mornings, your laughter, your rituals, your dreams. You love the woman who learned to find balance between partnership and personhood. You see that love was never supposed to complete you, it was supposed to witness your becoming. And even if he never changes the way you hoped, you did. And that's what saved the story.

The Peace That Stays

Peace used to feel fragile, something you had to protect from people, moods, or missteps. Now it feels anchored. It's the quiet in your bones, the confidence that no matter what happens, you'll handle it. Because peace isn't the absence of pain, it's the presence of perspective. You've learned that peace doesn't always fix what's broken. Sometimes, it teaches you how to live beautifully anyway. You didn't choose easy, you chose evolution. And evolution is the real happily ever after.

The Blessing of Becoming

So here's your benediction, your soft closing prayer:

"May I never rush my healing.
May I never forget how far I've come.
May I build homes in peace, not pain.
May I honor the woman who stayed, and the one who still dreams of more.
May I continue to choose myself, even when I choose to stay."

Because in the end, becoming isn't about changing who you are. It's about remembering who you've been all along and finally having the peace to live her truth out loud.

REFLECTION PROMPTS FOR THE READER:

What does "becoming" mean to me now that I've survived the storm?

____

____

____

How can I honor my peace daily without guilt?

____

____

____

What version of me is emerging, and what does she need to thrive?

____

____

____

How do I want to love differently, now that I understand what peace costs and creates?

____

____

____

Affirmation

"I am the woman I prayed to become. My peace is not the ending, it's the inheritance. I am both the promise and the proof."

Fatima's "Peace Page" Version

My peace is not fragile. It's familiar now.

I've learned that peace doesn't come from everything being perfect; it comes from finally knowing what I will no longer fight for.

I no longer chase closure.
I no longer negotiate my intuition.
I no longer shrink to fit someone's comfort zone.

Peace is not passive for me anymore. It's a practice, a rhythm that shows up every time I choose silence over chaos, calm over control, and joy over judgment. I forgive myself for what I tolerated while I was still learning how to love myself better. I bless the lessons that taught me discernment disguised as heartbreak. And I honor the woman I've become; softer, wiser, and still full of light. I am no longer waiting for peace to find me.

I am the peace.
I am the home.
I am the whole prayer, answered and unfolding in real time.

Love,

— Fatima Anne

Fatima's "Becoming Page" Version

Peace isn't a finish line. It's my foundation now.

I've made a home inside myself that doesn't collapse when love feels uncertain.

I've stopped auditioning for comfort because I am the comfort.

I've stopped waiting for softness because I live softly.

I've stopped chasing validation because I am the proof.

Becoming isn't about perfection; it's about peace with progress.

And I'm proud of the woman I am becoming: faithful, grounded, free.

Love,

— Fatima Anne

Your Peace & Becoming

Who am I becoming? What does my peace look like? How can I reclaim it? What do I forgive myself for? What lessons am I keeping? What does Peace mean to me now? What is my affirmation for this next chapter? What is my daily promise to myself?

"Peace is not what I find, it's what I protect."

"Becoming is the blessing."

A LOVE LETTER
the Woman Who Stayed

For the woman who stayed,
not out of weakness, but out of wisdom.

You thought healing would mean leaving.
But instead, you learned to see clearly.

You grieved the dream.
You honored the truth.

And somewhere along the way...
You found yourself again.

Now, if you stay, you stay differently.
With awareness. With boundaries. With peace.

This was never just about love.
It was about return.
You didn't lose love.
You just stopped losing yourself in it.
And that...
is everything.

Love,

— Fatima Anne

The Soundtrack of Potential

Curated by Caramel Xpressions

This playlist moves through the same journey as the book:
love, loss, clarity, and self-return.

From the quiet moment you feel something shift, to the truth
you can no longer ignore, to the peace you finally choose for
yourself.

Each song holds a version of you: the one who stayed, the one
who questioned, and the one who came back home.

This book was written with music in its bones.
Press play. Let it meet you where you are.